"As his pastor, knowing Nathan Lambshead has given me a unique opportunity to see into the heart of this man. I have seen a very deep faith that is the core of who he is. Nathan speaks from a place of learning the secret of working out your salvation, that Christ would be all in all."

Benjamin Swan
Pastor, Monadnock Full Gospel Church,
Rindge, New Hampshire

"After reading *Withstanding The Storm*, I believe Nathan has found keys to a deeper relationship with our Lord, that Jesus walks through the storms with us on many different levels."

Donner Roberson,
Beautiful Thunder Ministry,
Kiefer, Oklahoma

WITHSTANDING THE
STORM

Becoming the Christian You were Meant to Be

NATHAN LAMBSHEAD

TATE PUBLISHING *& Enterprises*

"Withstanding the Storm" by Nathan Lambshead
Copyright © 2006 by Nathan Lambshead. All rights reserved.
Published in the United States of America
by Tate Publishing, LLC
127 East Trade Center Terrace
Mustang, OK 73064
(888) 361-9473

Book design copyright © 2006 by Tate Publishing, LLC. All rights reserved.

No part of this publication may be reproduced, stored in a retrieval system or transmitted in any way by any means, electronic, mechanical, photocopy, recording or otherwise without the prior permission of the author except as provided by USA copyright law.

Scripture quotations marked "NASB" are taken from the *New American Standard Bible*®, Copyright © 1960, 1962, 1963, 1968, 1971, 1972, 1973, 1975, 1977, 1995 by The Lockman Foundation. Used by permission. All rights reserved.

Scripture quotations marked "KJV" are taken from the *Holy Bible, King James Version*, Cambridge, 1769.

Scripture quotations marked "NIV" are taken from the *Holy Bible, New International Version*®, Copyright © 1973, 1978, 1984 by International Bible Society. Used by permission of Zondervan Publishing House. All rights reserved.

Scripture quotations marked "ESV" are taken from *The Holy Bible: English Standard Version*, Copyright © 2001, Wheaton: Good News Publishers. Used by permission. All rights reserved.

This book is designed to provide accurate and authoritative information with regard to the subject matter covered. This information is given with the understanding that neither the author nor Tate Publishing, LLC is engaged in rendering legal, professional advice. Since the details of your situation are fact dependent, you should additionally seek the services of a competent professional.

ISBN: 1-5988640-7-6

Trust in the Lord with all your heart, lean not on your own understanding, in all your ways acknowledge Him, and He will make your paths straight.
Proverbs 3:5, 6 NIV

Dedicated to the memory of my parents, Charles Frederick and Marjory Ann. Mom and Dad, thank you for your dedication and faithfulness, to the Lord, to your children, and to each other. Thank you for your guidance, your love, your devotion, and the upbringing you gave us. This book is a tribute to you. Enjoy each other in the presence of our Lord in glory, and keep a watch out for me—I will be coming with my family to join you one day.

Your loving son,

Nathan

Table Of Contents

Foreword 11

Introduction........................ 13

Chapter One - The Foundation............. 27

Chapter Two - The Wall of Thanksgiving...... 33

Chapter Three - The Wall of Worship 43

Chapter Four - The Wall of Grace........... 49

Chapter Five - The Wall of Tithe............ 67

Chapter Six - The Roof of Fellowship 81

Summary 85

Authors Note 89

Epilogue........................... 93

Biography.......................... 97

Foreword

In *Withstanding the Storm*, Nathan dramatically contrasts Israel's journey into the Promised Land with his own life's wilderness experience. Using the parable of the wise and foolish builders found in Matthew, Chapter 7, Nathan re-enforces the importance of having a "solid rock" foundation before we begin work on our spiritual homes, by helping us to understand the "blueprints" for our lives that were created by the Grand Master Builder from the beginning of time.

In this, his first published book, Nathan provides us with materials necessary for building a spiritual home that will withstand the many storms of life. In it, you will find step-by-step instructions on how to build and maintain attitudes that make up the walls of our spiritual homes.

It is my prayer that who ever reads this "letter to a friend" humbly written by Nathan, will aptly apply it to their lives, so that when the rains come, the streams rise and the winds blow and beat against their spiritual dwelling place, they will remain safe in their house built upon the Rock.

Elizabeth A. Narkum

Introduction

Beginning as a letter to a friend, this book has developed into a teaching the Lord has put on my heart, through my own experiences in life. In it I talk about how we can end up not living the Christian life the way we should. Some people do not seem to have a problem with living the Christian life, while others do not seem to have what it takes to be consistent and to mature spiritually. For most of my life, the latter has been true for me. I never seemed to be able to overcome the cares of life, the worries of life, or the circumstances of life, consistently. I have been a "church goer" for most of my life and have heard thousands of sermons, many of which were Holy Spirit inspired for daily living. They just did not sink in, at least not in a life changing way. I would get excited at times and make a decision to change my ways, but along would come Monday and all would go back to the way it was before. It has so often been a struggle just to maintain love, joy, peace, and other fruit of the Spirit that should be present in the life of a follower of Jesus Christ. I would go through periods of time walking close to the Lord, excited about God and His life in me, then a change would come over me and I would lose my joy, my peace, and my enthusiasm for the things of God.

Love, peace, joy, patience, long suffering, being a person of prayer, reading God's Word daily, being a man or woman of faith, all of these things should be evident and continual if the Spirit of the living God is in you. So often in my life I have found the fruit of God's Spirit lacking in me. People would irritate, annoy, or offend me. I would have no inner peace or joy. I would worry about things. I would be discontent with what I had. I would envy others, and I would be very impatient. When I would try to pray, it was often like talking to a wall, therefore, I did not pray much. Reading the Bible was often pointless as well. I could read the same passage thirteen times and get nothing from it, or worse, get nothing but condemnation from it.

I have even questioned my very salvation more than once because I know this is not how the Christian life should be.

I would ask myself, "Why is it so hard for me? Why can't I be like other Christians?" A few years ago I came to the realization that I had better do something about the state I was in. If I should die, or if Jesus were to come again, I would not be prepared.

I came to the conclusion that nobody else was going to fix my life for me. I know that sounds pretty basic, but I had never really thought about it. I was living my life the same way, day after day, with no change. Before long, twenty years had gone by as quick as a heartbeat. I have now learned to analyze what I am doing and to consider my actions, and make wisdom-based decisions whether or not to carry on in the same manner, rather than just go on day after day without thought to my actions. Often I find that if I take the time to contemplate an issue, I can see whether or not I have been acting wisely or foolishly.

I know that I am responsible for my own life, including my spiritual walk, but without ever thinking about it, I just went on day after day without growth or victory. Maybe you can identify with some of these issues I am talking about.

I was raised as a missionary kid in a God-fearing, God-serving home. Subconsciously, I have been relying on my parent's spirituality and their walk with God to get me through life. Foolishness when I take the time to actually think about it, but that was exactly how I was living. I also realized I had been subconsciously behaving this way with various pastors, elders and youth leaders that I have been involved with over the last 30 years.

A while ago the Lord put the parable about the wise man and the foolish man from Matthew chapter seven on my heart.

> Therefore everyone who hears these words of mine and puts them into practice is like a wise man who built his

house on the rock. The rain came down, the streams rose, and the winds blew and beat against that house; yet it did not fall, because it had it's foundation on the rock. But everyone who does not put these words into practice is like a foolish man who built his house on the sand. The rain came down, the streams rose, and the winds blew and beat against that house, and it fell with a great crash.

(Matthew 7:24–27 NIV)

I have read that parable many times, and have heard many teachings on it. This time, however, I was hearing it in my spirit. The real me was listening. As I studied and chewed over this parable for some time, it became clear to me that it was not the building of his house on the rock that made the wise man wise, but it was fear and respect for the storm that made him wise. For the wise man, building his house on the rock was the result of wisdom. If no storm were coming, it would be foolishness to build on the rock. It puts me in mind of the scripture:

The man without the Spirit does not accept the things that come from the Spirit of God, for they are foolishness to him, and he cannot understand them, because they are spiritually discerned.

(I Corinthians 2:14 NIV)

Let's consider these two men, each of equal resources, building their own house. One builds his house on the beach, shaping it any way he wants, using all of his available materials. The other must go through the pain and hard work of hauling what he can up to the rock. He will have to shape his house to the rock instead of building it the way he would like, leaving some of his building materials behind. Nothing about this seems wise. Of course, we know the rest of the story. The storm! Before you continue reading, I am going to ask you one thing–do you believe in the storm? If you do not believe that anything terrible can happen to you, then reading this book may be a waste of your time. If you do believe it, you may realize deep down inside that the time has come for you to build before it is too late. For me it was an easy decision because I believed in the storm. I have seen and experienced many of life's storms. Some of them minor, some of them major, with any one of them having the power to take me out, especially when they accumulate. Having traveled the world fairly extensively earlier in my life, often to third world countries, I have seen things that are almost unheard of here in the United States. Circumstances and conditions people have to endure that seem inhuman. There are big storms occurring outside our borders that we in America are often not very aware of. Places where even today Christians are being persecuted, imprisoned, enslaved, and murdered for their faith. These men and women know what it is like to be in the midst of a real storm. The Word of God tells us that in the last days a time is coming that is worse than any time that was before.

> ... There will be a time of distress such as has not happened from the beginning of nations until then ...
>
> (Daniel 12:1 NIV)

We have recently experienced tragic storms like the Tsunami that hit so many countries, and Hurricane Katrina on our own coast, that have left people and families completely devastated. Many were not prepared for anything like that, physically, emotionally, or spiritually. Many have also suffered other circumstances like cancer or some other terrible affliction, or living under a regime like Nicholi Caicesque, Sadam Hussein, or the Taliban in Afghanistan. For them, knowing that a time is coming that will be worse than has ever been suffered before must be unimaginable. It is a storm that most of us cannot fathom. If we are unable to overcome the normal storms of life, how can we even hope to survive that kind of storm?

I came to realize that I was in no shape to face anything of such magnitude. No wonder the Word of God says that in the last days some will fall away.

> But the Spirit explicitly says that in latter times some will fall away from the faith, paying attention to deceitful spirits and doctrines of demons,
>
> (I Timothy 4:1 NASB)

This scripture is addressing born-again Christians. The only time that you can fall away from something is if you were first a part of it. If you are walking along the side a house, you can't fall off the roof, because you need to be walking on the roof in order to fall off the roof. This scripture rebuffs the theory that "once you've said the sinner's prayer, there is no way you can lose it" (God does not take away our free will once we get saved) as well as another false belief that states "God would never let us suffer anything like that!" We tend to say or think things like this while these very persecutions are going on worldwide. We have the wrong mindset when we think that we are immune to it somehow, that God is only on our side and not theirs. "Nothing like that can happen to me." we think to ourselves, if only subconsciously.

This kind of thinking is nothing more than the enemy's tactics to lull us to sleep. To keep us lazing around in our beach homes, living life the way we like. I am not an alarmist. This is just reality.

After coming to the realization that I needed to build my house on the Rock, I had to figure out how to do it. Once the storm is here, I won't be able to go the Pastor's house or my parents' house for shelter. This is not like the story of the three pigs. If the enemy blows down your foundationless house, you can't run next door to your pastor and live in his house.

The 'house' that needs to be strong in times of storm, is referring to our own individual walk with the Lord. Our spiritual being. Our real self that will live for eternity. This one is not a family house, or a group home.

I do not want this letter to be full of parables or illustrations that are nice, but provide no practical application of how to put them to use. For myself I need a working knowledge of what to do in my everyday life, not just a lot of great sayings and illustrations. In this letter I am going to share with you my own personal experience of how to build a house that will stand.

Some time ago my hobby was the shotgun sport of trap shooting. I had been struggling a lot with some of the wider angled targets. I would listen to every good competitor and tried everything they said, but still I seldom broke more than eighty clay targets out of a hundred. One day, while casually talking to another competitor at the range, he said something that 'clicked' with me.

He said "There are no such things as straightaway targets. They are ALL angled."

Within two weeks my average was up to ninety eight percent, and I was breaking the targets with ease. Somehow what he said, or the way he had said it, had turned me around. That proved to me that sometimes all you need is to hear someone else's approach to a problem or issue and it can set you on the path to victory, even if you have heard the same truth many times from other people who presented it in different ways.

God has been showing me, step by step, where the problems lay with my inconsistent growth and lack of maturity. Individual issues are easy to resolve by specific teachings relating to the problem, but the constant waxing back and forth and being inconsistent is another story. Something is fundamentally wrong when you can't be consistent in your spiritual life. For a time you may be on fire for God and at peace with the Lord, then before you realize it, something is wrong. You are becoming disappointed and disillusioned, eventually even resentful and bitter. You have negative words and feelings about people and circumstances. You are miserable, and it is usually without ever realizing or acknowledging it, even to yourself. You may step down from what you are doing at church, start to look for a different church, or even stop going to church altogether. You may even seek the company of others that have the same issues and opinions.

The Lord showed me that this is a direct result of an attitude problem. Attitudes will affect your actions. Neither the Devil nor God gives us these attitudes. They are something we have dominion over. God has given us control over our attitudes.

God has also led me through some basic attitude restructuring that I needed to work on in order to build my spiritual house. It is a simple house; a foundation, four walls and a roof, all built on His Word. Our spiritual house is more like a brick house than a wooden one. It is built for the most part in layers, piece by piece and row by row. The rest of the house, the internal rooms, interior decorating and improvements, is an ongoing story. Those parts of the building project never will end in this life.

There will always be improvements and remodeling, so to speak, but these structural 'attitudes' must be put up and kept up in order to stand.

You do not need to be a priest, nor have a degree from a Bible College to understand and to interpret the fundamentals of God's Word. God's basic life structures are very clear and there can be no mistaking the meaning. All you need is to be serious about building your house, and seek Him by reading His Word.

I pray this teaching will help you as it continues to help me.

Chapter One

The Foundation

First and foremost comes the foundation.

In this illustration, the rock is not the foundation, but rather the common ground for all houses to be built upon. It is the Word of God. The unchanging, uncompromising, everlasting, living Word of God that you can absolutely depend on. No storm can take out this rock.

Every home needs its own individual foundation to keep it anchored on the rock. A house without a foundation will get blown off the rock, while those with a foundation will stand. That foundation is: Do it God's way. I know it sounds simple, but I believe it is the most important thing for us to learn and to take seriously. This is how to " … seek first the Kingdom of God and His righteousness, and all these things will be added to you" (Matthew 6:33 KJV)–you need to seek to do it God's way. As teenagers, this is tough because we think we know everything, and as adults it can also be tough, because even though we discovered we do not know everything, we have been through a lot, learned a lot, and come to trust in our own experience and judgment. This does not mean that we are to stop using the brain God gave us and to stop learning from our past, but we still need to learn to do it God's way, based on His Word, and to stop depending on our own knowledge or experience. In everything we do acknowledge God by doing it His way. (Proverbs 3:5, 6) In every single aspect of your daily decision making, be sure it is what Jesus would do if He were walking the planet today. This is easy because His Spirit living in you lets you know right away what His way is if you are serious. "My sheep hear my voice …" (John 10:27 KJV)

Here are some simple examples that show us that God's way, the right way, is very obvious.

- Ignoring your five-year-old son who wants Daddy's attention, just because you are too busy right now, even though you know that what you are busy with can wait—Is that what Jesus would do? No.
- Tearing down somebody's effort or ministry within the church that disagrees with your ideas—Is that God's way? No.
- Not paying a debt to a business or credit card company, just because they really can't do anything about it, and after all you don't have the money and you need to give offerings to the church right?—Is that Jesus would have done? No.
- Flirting with that girl from the office, (after all the two of you have such strong 'feelings' for each other)—Is that what Jesus would do? No.
- Not telling someone about Jesus and His redemptive work on the cross when you are given the perfect

opportunity—Is that what God would have you do? No.

If you stop and really consider what Jesus would do in any particular situation, the answer is undeniably obvious. He would put aside His own busy-ness for his son. He would never hinder somebody's ministry or service. He would pay His debts in full and keep His word of agreement to all. He would not seek to flirt with that girl from the office, but would rather seek the opportunity to lead her to salvation.

The right way, God's way, needs to become our foundation in every choice we make, large or small.

I love to read the Old Testament. I find it to be a revelation of who God is and how He works. One thing I am amazed by is how the lives of the Israelites mirror our own spiritual life. How it mirrors our own walk with God. As we read about the lives of the Israelites, especially when they occupied the Promised Land, we see how they would continue for a generation or so, worshipping Jehovah and keeping His commandments, and would be prosperous, fruitful, and stand mighty against their enemies. Then along would come a new generation. This generation would neglect God's commandments. They would erect idols and worship false gods. Every time, without fail, down they would fall. They would suffer famine and pestilence and be conquered and consumed by their enemies. God would rise up a man or woman to deliver them, they would repent and turn back to God, and all would be restored. This never failed to happen, but they did not learn from their past. We need to learn from their past.

To sum it up: God's way, not our way. He can't stand with you if you are in disobedience. He would not be a God who loves you, and He does love you. He will never forsake you, but He also can't bless you and keep you while you are in disobedience. It is in our sinful natures to get worse and worse if there is no consequence to our actions. God traveled with the Israelites for forty years in the desert, never forsaking them, but there was no deliverance to the Promised Land as long as they behaved the way they did. He was on the side of the Israelites in blessings and prosperity when they obeyed Him and kept His commandments. Doing everything God's way keeps us on course.

It is very common to see a new believer start out on fire for God, excited about their rebirth and Christianity, only to grow cold and fall away with time. The attitude adjustments, which I will be referring to as walls, are very easy to build and maintain. They will absolutely change your outlook and your consistent growth in the Lord, and turn the storms of life into mere breezes.

Chapter Two

The Wall of Thanksgiving

The first attitude that you want to build your home with is the Wall of Thanksgiving.

Some time ago, I was contemplating the verse "In everything give thanks…" (I Thessalonians 5:18 KJV)

The first thing that came to my mind was "Yeah right! You can't thank Him for everything!" but as I chewed on it, the Word started to become clearer to me. It says in everything to give thanks, not for everything. Obviously we don't give thanks for bad things. We can, however, give thanks in all things, whether good or bad. In other words, in all situations and circumstances, we can give thanks to God. There are no promises in the Word that state we are not going to go through tough and stormy times. Jesus Himself said,

> I have told you these things, so that in me you may have peace. In this world you will have trouble. But take heart! I have overcome the world.
>
> (John 16:33 NIV)

I came to realize, after really contemplating this, that I was not a man of thanksgiving. I did not have a grateful heart. I had quite the opposite. I was hardly ever satisfied with what I had, always envying others, and so often feeling sorry for myself. That sounds pretty disgusting, but the sinful nature does stink, and I was born into it. We all were born into it, and can experience an ungrateful heart to some degree.

I remember experiencing a heavy feeling of regret that I had lived my life for so long this way. My Lord Jesus came to this earth and was born as a man. He served, suffered, died, and rose again from the grave for me. I am His bride, an heir to the Kingdom. Why then was I going around feeling sorry for myself? Why did I constantly envy what others had and was never satisfied with what I had? The answer was quite simple: because I did not have the wall of thanksgiving up in my life. Instead, I had built a wall of bitterness and envy up in my beach house, on the sand.

In the same way that the Israelites so often turned to idols, I found that I was worshipping the idol of self. I asked the Lord to show me how to overcome this stronghold, and He did. He challenged me to find something to be thankful about in every one of the circumstances that I faced. To give thanks in every feeling or emotion I went through, and in everything I saw or read about others going through as well.

For a period of time whenever I had a free moment to think, giving thanks is what I would think about. God's voice speaking to my inner spirit helped me. I came up with things I couldn't have imagined. Here are some examples of where God led me:

1. At work, when blamed by co-workers, or even my boss, for something I have no control over, and

knowing I had done my best, I learned to thank God that He knows all about it and He stands with me. I remember how Jesus stood in front of Pilot; accused of everything He was not guilty of and said nothing. When challenged by Pilot, He said: "You would have no power over me if it were not given to you from above. Therefore the one who handed me over to you is guilty of a greater sin." (John 19:11 NIV) I can thank God that He knows I am not guilty. God put my boss in the position he is in, and He stands with me before my accusers. I can thank God that He is my truth and my justice. I can also be thankful that I actually have a job.

2. Even though I drive the smallest, oldest, most weather-beaten car in the parking lot, I can thank Him that it is paid for and that I do not have to work a couple of days each week just to make a payment on it. I thank Him that my car gets 45 MPG and is reliable. I remembered how having a new car is great for a while, but pretty soon the excitement wears off and the years of debt become the reality.

3. When ridden at work about my 'religious nonsense,' I can thank Him that He considers me worthy of taking that ridicule for Him. I thank Him for the treasure He is storing up for me because of it.
4. I thank Him when it seems I never have money for what I want. (Even though I know that what I want is not always good for me.) He knows what's best for me, like a shepherd does for his sheep. I can thank Him that I am one of His sheep.

This exercise went so far that once, after a successful bowel movement, I was moved to thank Him. My first reaction was, "Well, this is not very reverent! This is going too far!"

He reminded me right away of what it can be like when not successful in this area. I was humbled quickly, and thanked him for His goodness, and the health He has given me. That bowel movement, I realized, was actually to His glory. He created me, and His creation was working the way He intended. How could I question that? It was a revelation to me of the reality of God. It is so easy to cloud our concept of God with religious ideas and perceptions. He is concerned with every single part of us.

The Wall of Thanksgiving is one where you often need to look at others, and get your eyes off yourself. If you are feeling sorry for yourself for something that you do not have, or because of some circumstance you are facing, I can guarantee that if you look around you will find somebody who has a lot less, or who is going through a lot worse. You can thank God you are not as bad off as they are. It could always be a lot worse.

This exercise is still on-going in my life, but after a short while I realized that I was set free of the self-pity, envy, misery, and dissatisfaction that an ungrateful and thankless heart produces. I do not need to try to find ways to thank Him any more, as it is now a part of my new nature. I do find, however, as with everything else that it takes maintenance. The Wall of Thanksgiving can't be eroded by the storm, but it can break down from internal neglect.

We have all observed kids complaining at Christmas

time: "I didn't get what I wanted!" or "She got more than I did!" This is an attitude we need to 'teach' out of them, any way possible. We have all met adults who did not learn this either. They are miserable, thankless people, basically useless to society, and definitely ineffective in the Kingdom of God while in this condition. I absolutely believe in our Lord's ability to set us free and deliver us, but I have seldom seen a lack of thankfulness completely overcome. This enemy stronghold is actually idolatry, worshipping the idol of self. A grateful person, one who is full of thanksgiving, and who can thank God in all circumstances, will be unable to worship the idol of self at the same time. This is a true instance of light and darkness not being able to occupy the same place at the same time. "…what fellowship can light have with darkness?" (II Corinthians 6:14 KJV)

So many of the enemy's strongholds will vanish once the Wall of Thanksgiving goes up.

The Israelites had ungrateful hearts. They were given so much. Manna from heaven, water from rocks, pillars of fire by night and clouds by day as guides in the wilderness. The list goes on and on, but Israel was forever murmuring and being ungrateful. When they erected idols the grace of God left them. He was no longer in their corner so to speak, and would leave them to their own devices. Worshipping the idol of self is no different. "What agreement is there between the Temple of God and idols?" (II Corinthians 6:16 KJV)

If you live with the misery that the idolizing of self brings, you can be taken out by the least of storms the enemy sends your way. It is his business to take you out. He is good at it, but he can only use what you allow him to. If you are to present the Devil the wall of selfishness, ungratefulness, and self-worship, he will have no problem taking you down. However, the misery and bitterness of an ungrateful and covetous heart will simply no longer exist as long as you are actively thanking the Lord in everything.

The "Joy of the Lord" is the fruit that thankfulness helps to develop within us. The fruit of joy that God gives us is not the same as the selfish 'happiness' that the world chases after.

Living with the joy of the Lord in your heart will give you a peaceful, victorious life that allows you to become a person of true worship.

Chapter Three

The Wall of Worship

The second attitude is the Wall of Worship. It is very close to the Wall of Thanksgiving. So close in fact, that they can be built up together.

God led me in a little different direction in this lesson. It was not how to worship, or where to worship, or why to worship. It was when to worship.

As we read the story of the Israelites, we see how crossing the Red Sea was the first big obstacle they faced in exiting the bondage of Egypt. There was a body of water in front of them that they could not cross, and the Army of Pharaoh behind them, ready to defeat them and take them back to captivity. We know how it went … God, through His servant Moses, parted the water and Israel walked through the sea as though it were dry land. After the last Egyptian soldier behind them stepped into the parted Red Sea, God closed up the water around them, causing the Egyptian army to drown, delivering the Israelites from their enemy. I can only imagine how Israel felt as they danced with joy and sang praise and worship to Jehovah once they saw how God defeated their enemies!

It was a good thing that they acknowledged God for what He had done, but as I considered the story in its entirety, I realized that the thanksgiving and worship that was offered up to God at that time really meant nothing. Israel was worshipping God on the wrong side of the water!

The Israelites needed to be worshipping God on the side of the sea that was facing the problem. When they were facing their storm they needed to be praising God. I have to be sympathetic to their plight. I know I would have joined them in murmuring and worrying. If my family and all we owned were in that situation, I would be beside myself with worry and doubt, and would probably be blaming Moses for everything.

I have come to realize that murmuring is actually a form of devil worship. When worshipping God, we state who He is, what He has done, how we love Him, and we give Him all the glory, honor, and praise. When murmuring, we are repeating all of the bad things that the enemy, Satan, is authoring or using to destroy us. We are actually giving honor to it in a distorted way. The challenge in building the Wall of Worship is to stay in a place of worship when all is going wrong. Worship Him when you least feel like it. Worship God when you are faced with the storm, whatever your storm may be.

When something arises and your first instinct is to complain, worry, blame somebody else, murmur, and basically honor the devil in it, then is the time to raise your voice in worship. Lift your heart and your countenance toward Him, your Creator, the Lord your God. Give Him glory and worship Him in spite of it all. When you get past the storm, and you will, and are in a state of elation at your deliverance, you will then be a true worshipper. A true disciple of Jesus, and not just a mere believer.

The church today has many people in the congregation who do not know when to worship. Only when all is going right can they worship God. When the kids are behaving the way they should, when their spouse is loving them just right, when they have a fat bank account, when business is good, when the Pastor preaches the messages they want to hear, when the worship teams plays the songs they like, then they can worship God.

If you find that this is the only time you can worship the Lord your God, then you are not a true worshipper in spirit, because your worship does not go deeper than the natural level. In a sense, without realizing it, you are only worshipping your good circumstances, not God. Therefore if your circumstances are not good, you can't worship God.

This may sound harsh, but it is the condition of many believers today. I found myself to be in the condition of being unable to worship in the midst of a bad situation. The Wall of Worship is a wall I have only just begun to build. I probably have a few rows of bricks laid. I often forget to worship in the midst of the situation and blow it, but when I choose to worship God instead, the selfish, ungrateful, angry, worried feelings I get simply vanish.

Keep in mind that the storm could be a real attack, like disease or persecution, or it may only be something like the car breaking down on your way to work, or a fight with your spouse. Anything that gets you in a bad mood, a mood that you can't worship the Lord in. That is the time to worship.

Again I want to point out that light can't be in the same place as darkness. Turn on the light of worship, and the darkness, the form of 'devil worship' that murmuring is, will flee. The gates of hell and the storms of hell will not prevail against your house.

It is interesting how God used the very obstacle, the Red Sea, to deliver Israel from their enemy. Often the obstacle or circumstance we see in the natural, God uses for us, if we have faith in Him, and do not succumb to the lies of the enemy.

> …All things work together for the good for them that love God, and are called according to His purpose.
>
> (Romans 8:28 KJV)

Pharaoh would have plagued them in their journey to the Promised Land if he had not been taken out. God used the very obstacle confronting Israel to deliver them once and for all from the army of darkness.

The Wall of Worship produces an overcoming faith, as well as peace, patience, longsuffering, and the ability to trust God in all things and for all things. Your life will be an example to others, and an encouragement to God's children.

Chapter Four

The Wall of Grace

The third attitude is the wall of Grace. The Wall of Grace is where you absolutely take your eyes off everyone else and put them on yourself. Be concerned with your own house only, no others.

I think we have all heard these words: "You call yourself a Christian and you do …" or: "They call themselves priests and they …" or maybe: "If there was a God, why would He allow … ?"

Maybe you have even found yourself speaking these words. This is a result of walking in judgment. The world is sitting in the seat of judgment in their lives, while we are sitting in the seat of grace, or at least we should be sitting there. We need to learn how to stay in the seat of grace. We need to learn how to forgive without question and without condition. In the past, I have found myself looking at others, especially in the church, and thoughts would go through my mind about how they may act while there, because I happen to know how they act elsewhere during the week.

Is it any wonder why the church is fighting ineffectiveness and a lack of power, when this type of judgment is going on amongst ourselves? I know how much I myself have acted this way, and how often I hear others talking the same way. It is more prevalent than we realize.

The Wall of Grace is very important. The Word has plenty of teaching on this.

> Do not judge, or you too will be judged. For in the same way you judge others, you will be judged, and with the measure you use, it will be measured to you.
>
> (Matthew 7:1, 2 NIV)

Therefore you have no excuse, everyone of you who passes

judgment, for in that which you judge another, you condemn yourself; for you who judge practice the same things.

(Romans 2:1 NASB)

We need to take this Word from God to heart. Remember the major difference between us and the world is the measurement God uses to judge us. The blood of Jesus is the only thing separating us from the world. When God's hand of judgment comes to the born-again believer, it passes over. He does not see us, but the blood of Jesus, His blood, covering us. While the world is pointing their finger at us, God, the REAL judge, is pointing His finger at the world. It is a judgment that the world cannot escape. When the people of the world point their fingers at us, often what they say is absolutely true. We are not perfect. That is why we need grace. That is why we need to be forgiven, just as they themselves need to be forgiven. This is fundamental, but we tend to forget it.

Passing judgment on others causes bitterness and a

lack of love in our lives. God has commanded us, not asked us, to love one another.

> A new command I give you: Love one another. As I have loved you, so you must love one another.
>
> (John 13:34 NIV)

Judging causes us to be offended by others. Christians being offended by one another is one of the biggest problems that cause the individual, and the church as a whole, to be held back and ineffective.

The thing to remember here is that most of the time we do not know the whole truth and our reaction is based on a false conclusion. This is the work of the Accuser.

We read about the Accuser in the book of Job, and he is still active today. He has not been thrown down–at least not yet. He is actively accusing everyone to each other, keeping us in a state of judgment and bitterness if we respond to it.

He accuses God to us (starting at the very beginning in the Garden, when he accused God of lying to Eve), he accuses Christians to sinners, Christians to each other, and even sometimes believers to God (as in the case of Job), and so often he also accuses us to our selves. We need to learn how to forgive ourselves the same way God has forgiven us. It keeps us from dwelling on our past and allows us to move on with the Lord.

I have operated in the realm of judgment a lot in my life. For years I have gone from church to church, allowing myself to become offended by one of the leaders or some other person there. Eventually I found myself living a completely backslidden life. This lasted quite a few years. I was completely disgusted by church and all of its going's on. "Jesus is cool; I can love Him, but not all of those Christians!" I would say.

If we can't love each other, how can the love of God be in us? (See 1 John 3:11–24)

This scripture passage always tore me up while living in a state of bitterness and resentment toward God's people. "How can I love someone that did ... to me?" I would say.

The attitude of judgment had a stranglehold on me for a long time. A few years ago I truly repented of my ways. I went back to church, got involved, and was hungry for His Word once more. I had made the 'prodigal son' journey back to the Lord, and He had accepted me with open arms. He delivered me from the pigsty of a backslidden, rebellious existence, and I was keeping His commandments once more. After a period of time, however, I came up against this same spirit in me, this spirit of judgment. I was about to throw out the work God had started to repair in me and said: "The heck with it. I want nothing to do with this church or these people anymore. Maybe I'll try another one…" when all of a sudden I 'saw' the accuser. It was almost as if I could see the enemy, Satan, standing there as he spoke to me. All I remember saying to him was this:

"Ha! You Liar! I see you now! I will not listen to you anymore. I don't care what someone has said or done, until God takes me out of this church I will stay. If I can't be involved in anything in the church because of these attitudes, so be it. I will just attend and do whatever God asks of me. I will not let you win anymore. You have done this to me long enough!" It seemed like a huge weight had lifted off me, a weight that had been hanging over me for a long time.

Learning to appropriate grace and to forgive others as He has forgiven you may not lead you to recognizing the Accuser's voice, but will give you victory over it, because the voice will no longer have any authority in your life. Even though you hear it, you will not act on it.

An example of how the Accuser can manipulate us when we listen to him will involve different circumstances or conditions, but it can often go something like this:

A young man, whom I will call Joe, got saved. It was a dramatic conversion. His family members were church going believers who prayed for him faithfully. It was seemingly hopeless that he would come to the Lord, but he did, and in a big way. He was very excited and turned on to the Lord. It was a big emotional event in his life. The church happened to be in the middle of a large project at the time that Joe was a big help in, as it was part of his area of expertise. The Pastor would often call him up to talk with him, pray with him, and discuss his life and family. They worked on the project together as well. Joe was being discipled by a caring shepherd.

When the project was finally done, Joe had to miss a Sunday service for legitimate reasons, and the Pastor did not call him up that week. A bell started to ring in Joe's mind. He had to miss the following Sunday service as well, and once again, no call from the Pastor. Now Joe was putting voice to it inside. "Why hasn't the Pastor called me?" he thought.

He deliberately missed the next Sunday, and the Pastor did call this time. He called to ask Joe to come down to the church and help him with something! Now the voice was loud and clear inside Joe.

"All he does is use me! Now that the project is done, he does not call, and when he does call it is just because he needs something!" he would say to himself.

A seed of bitterness and accusation was taking root in Joe. He started to recall all the other things that offended him about his Pastor and other people in the church also. Today Joe does not go to church and he has become disillusioned. The great talent he has to offer and the great contribution he is capable of making is not happening. The excitement of serving God is gone. The peace and joy he experienced is being replaced with his old ways. His old ways are unsatisfactory to him now, however, and he does not understand why. Joe has lost his first love, and the excitement of serving the living God. That is the reason why things have changed for Joe. He does not understand how it happened, nor does he know how to get back what he lost.

Another example is one that I can take from my own experience. Since I play the guitar and sing, I am asked to lead a service in worship from time to time. It had been awhile since I had led a service in worship, when the Pastor asked me to lead a Good Friday night service. I was asked to lead the singing with some hymns, played solo on the guitar. These songs are difficult finger picking numbers, which I had not done in some time. I was also asked to sing a solo. The Lord put a song on my heart that I had never done before. The song was about His death on the cross, and the Lord led me to introduce it with speaking first, dramatically leading up to the nails being driven into His hands, then into the song itself. This is something I absolutely dreaded. I am NOT an actor or public speaker at all. Even way back in school I had a terrible time standing in front of the class to give a speech. I would rather face the playground bullies.

Well, I led the worship without a hitch in the tough songs I was asked to play, and I presented my speech and sang the song, and all went well. After the service I packed up my stuff and was on the way out when I saw the Pastor standing by the door. I expected him to thank me and tell me I did a good job, but he did not say a word.

I remember driving home thinking to myself that my whole effort was in vain. The Pastor did not appreciate what I went through to do this at all. I was never going to do it again, that much I knew! As I was driving along, however, the Lord started to get through to me. "Give him a chance" the Lord said. "Your pastor is a busy servant, with a very busy Easter weekend coming up." I listened, and just let go to what the Lord was saying to me. I remember thinking to myself, "Well, I did what the Lord asked of me, and He is pleased. Don't worry if nobody else realizes what you went through to do it." I felt a weight lift from off my shoulders, and had a great time of worship and extreme closeness with the Lord for the rest of the night.

Two days later, while practicing with the worship team for the Easter morning service, the pastor came up to me and apologized for not thanking me for the Friday night service, and that my music was very effective.

I had already gotten over it and put it behind me, but I recognized right then and there how so often in the past I had let my feelings take me down a completely different road, a road of resentment, bitterness, and disappointment.

The Accuser is the world's greatest liar, the father of lies. The best lie consists mainly of the truth, where often only the conclusion is the lie. The facts leading up to the conclusion can be absolutely true. The Accuser knows how to do this so well. Joe did not realize it, but the circumstances that led up to his problem were used by the Accuser to get him to this state of judgment and being offended. It was not his own voice he was hearing. The facts that led up to Joe's situation were true, but the conclusion was not true at all. The Pastor is a busy man, and at that particular time the demands on him were very high, with people pulling on him from every direction. He had not forgotten Joe. He cares very much for Joe. One of the ways a pastor disciples others is to let go a little at a time so that the person can start to grow on their own. The same way we let our children go, in stages. If Joe had stopped and really thought about it, and been honest with himself, he would have known this to be true. The enemy just used Joe's circumstances to create the lie. The facts leading up to the wrong conclusion for my own situation were true also. The pastor did not thank me at the end of the Good Friday service. However, that truth did not change the fact that he really did appreciate me, and my effort. He was busy with the burden of a lot of needy people, and a very challenging weekend, and let it slip. The Lord reminded Him and he came to me later and apologized for forgetting. The lie was the conclusion that I had been coming up with, the conclusion that the Pastor did not like or appreciate me.

The same day the pastor apologized to me, some other people, who do not normally speak to me often, came up to me and told me how much I had blessed them with my music. The Lord had used me, and I was getting ready to make the decision to never do it again because of the Accuser's lies!

This is how the Wall of Grace works. When something similar to what happened to me and to Joe happens to you, you do not act on it. I have found that when I overcome a situation like the one Joe faced, by just not acting on the 'feelings' but acting like it never happened, the real truth is revealed to me afterwards. Then I find out the real facts about what someone said or why they acted the way they did. I realize that my conclusion at the time was way off the mark, and my judgment of that person was wrong.

One reason the enemy is such a good liar is that he includes our own voice in our own minds, along with our emotional response with the lie. We think that it is we ourselves coming up with these responses. Sometimes we even think it is God talking to us, revealing someone else's sin or injustice. Hear me well; God does not accuse anyone else to you! If He has forgiven you of all that you are guilty of, would He then turn around and accuse someone else's sin or shortcomings to you? No! If you hear or feel this in any way shape or form, it is the Accuser. The Liar. Pay no heed to these thoughts and feelings, no matter how they make you feel. Remember, feelings are just part of your natural being, and respond to every voice or circumstance that comes your way.

We tend to give our feelings too much authority. God gave us feelings, yes. We can absolutely 'feel' God. However we can also 'feel' the Devil, and we can also 'feel' our own fallen nature. Learn to recognize this and it can set you free in many areas. We have to learn not to let our feelings govern our decisions.

There will also be times when you may experience very real offenses. Situations where someone is deliberately doing you wrong. This is an exciting time for me now. In the past I would be filled with indignation and bitterness, but inside I would know I was out of God's will. Now, however, I can forgive my accusers in the same manner God has forgiven me. I know my Lord says to me "well done" each time that happens. I seek those words more than anything else in this life.

On a side note to this subject, I have observed and experienced two of the tactics Satan uses if he can't stop you from getting saved and going to church:

Plan A: The Devil would like to pick the church for you to attend. You would stand a better chance of hearing a word from God in a saloon than in the church Satan chooses for you. At least there may be a salvation tract left in the bar, or someone witnessing about Jesus. The church that Satan would choose would keep you in ignorance and under a religious spirit. If that does not work, the Devil often has success with plan B.

Plan B is a much more subtle plan. He gets you to 'worship' church. Not in a conscious way, but subliminally, you end up following the church as an organization, or the pastor as a person, and you get your eyes off Jesus, the one you were looking at when you got saved in the first place. Your sense of spiritual well-being comes from how the pastor treats you, how he preaches, or how the church operates, rather than from the new life dwelling in you. Satan now has you under a religious spirit, even while attending a good church, and you don't even realize it.

The church, which is a body of human beings, and the pastor, who is also a human being, will let you down sooner or later. In so many cases this results in disappointment and disillusionment. This offended attitude causes you to grow cold. You lose your first love. This is the point when many believers go in search of another church, or worse, do not go to church at all, but go back, bit by bit, to the life they once led. If they do decide to go back to church, Satan can try Plan A again, and choose a church for them. If that does not work, he still has Plan B, where he keeps them operating with their eyes on man and off of God. As long as this is happening, they will never mature as disciples of Jesus.

The religious leaders of Jesus' time were guilty of

operating with their eyes on man. They worshipped the law, not the law giver. They were so blinded by 'religion' that they actually killed Jesus, the Son of God. We are all guilty of His death, since He died for all of us, but they are guilty of killing Him. That is a powerful demonstration of how destructive a religious spirit can be in your life.

Find a church to attend that is close enough to where you live, one that is a Bible teaching and Spirit filled body that you can get plugged into and become an active member of. Seek the Lord in prayer over your decision. He promises in His Word that those who seek Him shall find Him. Submit to those whom God placed in authority at that church, grow in your knowledge and your walk with the Lord, but never take your eyes off of Jesus, nor let the church or anyone else in it take His place in your heart. Always remember who your Savior is, who your Lord is, who your Peace is, who your Joy is, who your Counselor is, who your Fulfillment is, who your God is.

The fruit of love, God's love, is only possible when

we walk in Grace. It is tough to take pity on someone when you are offended by their very presence!

> This is how we know what love is: Jesus Christ laid down His life for us. We ought to lay down our lives for our brothers. If anyone sees a brother in need and has no pity on him, how can the love of God be in him?
>
> (I John 3:16, 17 NIV)

Forgiving is the heart of God, and we want the heart of God. We want to please God by being faithful to Him.

Chapter Five

The Wall of Tithe

The fourth attitude is the Wall of Tithe. This is the easiest wall of all, yet many stumble on it. It is different than the others, in that the first three walls, Thankfulness, Worship, and Grace, are attitudes that affect your actions. Tithing is the other way around. It is an action that will affect your attitude.

The difference between a tithing and a non-tithing believer is like the difference between someone who calls themself a patriot, and someone who joins the Army. Becoming obedient in tithe is like joining the Army of God.

I do not believe that we are under the Old Testament

law, but rather we are under the New Covenant. Some Christians, however, use that truth to teach that we no longer should tithe. Jesus did happen to say...

> Do not think that I have come to abolish the Law or the Prophets; I have not come to abolish them but to fulfill them. I tell you the truth, until heaven and earth disappear, not the smallest letter, not the least stroke of a pen, will by any means disappear from the Law until everything is accomplished.
>
> (Matthew 5:17, 18 NIV)

Jesus came and died for our sins, and on the cross He said "it is finished," and His redemptive work absolutely was finished. The war is won, but Heaven and Earth has not disappeared, and by no means has all been accomplished yet. His disciples were to spread the word to all the world. We also have to keep spreading the word to all the world. This takes money, as well as our obedience in answering the call He has on our lives to be a light to the world. If you think all has been accomplished, just look around you. This can't be it.

The word 'tithe' has for some taken on the meaning of law, and they can't see past it. Tithe does not mean law, it simply means a tenth, or ten percent. Ten percent is the figure God gave, and it is a perfect one to keep. I also like to call it giving, rather than tithing, but the word tithe is easy to understand. I personally do not believe that widows, orphans, elderly people on fixed incomes, etc. should be giving money they need to live on, but rather they should be receiving financial help from us, the Church. We need to keep the balance as God intended it. Most of us are in a position to tithe, however, and everyone, no matter what their position in life, is able to give of themselves in some way.

Having a lot of bills and not being able to afford to give, or some other excuse like that is deceptive thinking, and is not God's way. There is no faith or commitment in that. The money that the needy require should come from us, giving cheerfully, and not from government programs.

Something that happened to my parents back in the late 1960's while on the mission field in South Africa always stands out in my mind whenever I may wonder if I have enough money this week, or whether I should pay a tithe or keep it rather, in order to feed my family. My mother was in the kitchen, pondering whether or not to use some tithe money they had put in a jar for later, because they were completely out of money and had two growing boys to feed. The tithe was R15.00 (roughly eighteen dollars U.S. at the time) this could keep us in some basic staples and feed us for a couple of weeks back then. She was going back and forth in her mind about whether they should spend it or not. After all, God would understand, and they could pay it back later somehow. Right about then my Dad called out from the other room, and said that they had the 15.00 tithe money, but he did not think they should use it. That made up my mother's mind, and she said "ok, there's my answer. We won't use it." Immediately after she thought that, a knock came on the door, and a perfect stranger whom they had never met, and never saw again, handed them 15.00 and walked away. In a miraculous way God showed them that they were right to obey and to trust

Him. He loves us, and He will not let His children go hungry. "Trust and obey …" as the song says.

It is the attitude of giving and trusting fully in the Lord that is the important issue here. Money is very important to us. God knows this. The Bible has more than 2,300 verses that deal with money. God cares about our finances. He understands how much we need money. The financial storm that the enemy can bring is able to destroy you easier than almost anything else. Many of the problems in marriage also have their root in finances.

Whether you are the breadwinner of the family or not, I am sure you have no problem understanding that you definitely need God on your side in the area of finances.

I want to stress that we do not 'buy' god's blessing in any way. He loves us, just like we love our own children, unconditionally. In fact, far more so than we can even love our own children. Having a giving heart, is having God's heart. The new covenant He made with us is all about the heart attitude. Love as He has loved and you will fulfill the law. "Carry each other's burdens, and in this way you will fulfill the law of Christ." (Galatians 6:2 NIV)

Tithing is a first step toward carrying another's burdens for anyone who has never given of their finances, and who does not understand the concept. It is also a step towards trusting the Lord completely, and making a real commitment to Him. A step towards trusting in Him for your daily bread.

I have seen so many men of the world, even some Christians, who were very talented at making money. They seemed to have the world by the tail and life was good, just to lose it all overnight. We need to understand that we have no control over our circumstances. You are never in a 'safe' place financially. Thinking that you are financially safe is like lazing around in your hammock at your beach house, while the storm surge is coming.

I have attempted to tithe many times over the years, as I became of the age of independence. I just never seemed to succeed at it consistently. I was always short of cash. Never had the money I needed. There were always bills and expenses. Finally, a few years ago, I made a firm resolve that I was going to do it God's way, and I did not care if I went bankrupt doing it. I would not fail in this anymore! Not only have I not gone bankrupt since making this decision, but God has blessed me in so many ways I could not have imagined.

Rather than praying about how much to give each week, as I had been led to believe was the best way, by people in times gone past, I decided that God knows best, and made it ten percent of all that comes to me across the board, no matter what. This way I do not have to think, pray, or worry about how much to give in any way. God's way has kept me from the trap of thinking to myself that "this week I do not have enough," or wondering if I should give to this church because maybe they will not use the funds right, or any other excuse like that. His way is easy–"For my yoke is easy, and my burden is light" (Matthew 11:30 KJV).

We need God supporting us in the area of finances and holding up this wall of our house. He has made it clear that we have a choice, as in all things, to follow Him. To keep His commandments. We are stewards of all He gives us. I have heard it said that if all born again believers were faithful in tithing the church would be able to reach everyone in the world with money to spare. Isn't He coming again when all have heard?

Again, going back to the example of the Israelites, they needed to obey the Lord. Keeping everything to yourself and not tithing is the equivalent of worshipping a "golden calf." It is the very same idol represented by the one the Israelites erected and worshiped in the desert.

Tithing is a very real way of being able to show we truly trust in Him. It shows that we are true followers of the Almighty, and that this is not just some organization called church.

I have found that being faithful in tithe has set me free in more than one area. I can come before the throne of grace boldly, for I am an heir to that throne. I show it every time I write that check. I have confidence in the authority of the believer that He has given me, because I put my money where my mouth is.

I am not a man with a lot of money. My talents lay elsewhere, other than making money. I have a family to support and earn little compared to many, but I would put my God up against their bank account anytime. He has never failed to give us our daily bread. Our daily manna from heaven. We are also able to give in a fairly substantial way to the Kingdom of God on top of it. I find tithing helps to keep me trusting in Him all the time. I can never feel comfortable with the money I have put away. Trusting in Him rather than in my bank account is a very comfortable feeling to live with. Ten percent seems like a lot sometimes, but anytime I have kept it for myself instead, there was absolutely no change in my financial position in life. Since I made the decision to tithe I have seen God's hand in my finances in miraculous ways, and I can say that it really feels like I still have a Dad taking care of me, even though my parents have both gone on to be with the Lord now. Would I like to try being a millionaire? Sure. Who wouldn't? I personally think I could handle a big windfall better than anyone else. I would not let it get to me ... so I would like to think anyway.

I read a survey recently of lottery millionaires, and

it said that the suicide rate is up in that group compared to the financial group they were in before the winning ticket. How is that possible? The lies of the enemy, that's how. His lies about how 'happy' you would be with tons of money. How you would help the poor, help the church, do all these great things, and not let it ruin you. Again, learn to recognize Satan's voice.

There was another area of freedom I did not realize would come from this. Awhile back I was talking on the phone with someone I had called up who had left the church. He said something that shocked me. "One of the reasons I left is because the pastor talks about money so much!" I had to stop him there and ask if he was serious. I did not believe him. My wife had to confirm it for me. "Yes he does." she said. "Others have said so as well."

I had to sit back and think about that one. I could not respond right away to the person I had called. I came to realize that I have subconsciously learned to tune the pastor out when he starts on the subject of tithing. When he changes to the next subject I come right back to focus on what he is saying. I have learned to tune him out so well that I do not even recall him talking about money at all most of the time. I am not promoting ignoring the pastor. That is not God's way (remember the foundation). It is just that he is not talking to me when he brings up tithing, so I do not need to listen to him about this. It is like an alter call for salvation, in which I do not need to raise my hand or come forward, since I am already born again of His Spirit. I have been set free in the area of tithes and offerings in the same way, and have this God-wall up in my house. I am not saying that God can't move on me to give over and above ten percent, but He never has without me having it in the bank, or a promissory note on the way. He has never asked me to give of something I do not have in any area. I have found that I am always able to give the ten percent however. Who knows, maybe God actually knows what He is doing?

Unfortunately pastors everywhere are forced to talk about money. Believers are just not building this wall in their house. More is required from the few who do in order to make ends meet in so many churches. How can they possibly go beyond than their own four walls to reach out to the world? If someone doesn't talk about it, it just won't happen. Too bad it has to be the pastor. In times past the church has resorted to the terrible practice of making money by extortion, something that is still happening in some churches today. They make it a religious obligation in order for God to answer prayers and forgive sins. Not only is this the opposite of the heart of God, it also drives the world further away from the church, and rightfully so. Even in the days of Jesus we see a widow giving all she had.

> Jesus sat down opposite the place where the offerings were put and watched the crowd putting their money into the temple treasury. Many rich people threw in large amounts. But a poor widow came and put in two very small copper coins worth only a fraction of a penny. Calling his disciples to him, Jesus said, "I tell you the truth, this poor widow has put more into the treasury than all the others. They all gave out of their wealth; but she, out of her poverty, put in everything—all she had to live on.
>
> (Mark 12:41–44 NIV)

Jesus is teaching us that it is not the amount that is important, but it is the heart attitude. Can I ask you to tell me why she was giving all she had to the church however? This poor widowed woman should have been receiving financial help, not giving the little she had to live on.

> Religion that God our Father accepts as pure and faultless is this: to look after orphans and widows in their distress and to keep oneself from being polluted by the world.
>
> (James 1:27 NIV)

Another way to look at the finances of the church is this: Money needs to come from the outside. The pastor of the church is a tithing believer (at least true pastors are) but that does not help the church financially. The church is not a profit organization. I see tithing as being a way that I can be an essential part of the kingdom even though I am not in full time ministry like pastors, evangelists or missionaries. Somebody has to support them. The word says "anyone who receives a prophet because he is a prophet, receives a prophet's reward …"

(Matthew 10:41 NIV) Tithing is one way of receiving God's prophets.

God was not at all pleased with the children of Israel when they erected the golden calf, and neither is He pleased with us when we do the same. Put up this wall, the wall of tithe, keep it up and trust in Him with all your heart, lean not on your own understanding, in all your ways (and means) acknowledge Him!

God tells us in His Word that it is impossible to please Him without Faith.

> And without faith it is impossible to please God, because anyone who comes to him must believe that he exists and that he rewards those who earnestly seek him.
>
> (Hebrews 11:6 NIV)

Tithing alone will not produce great faith, but it is the beginning of becoming a man or woman of faith, a man or woman who pleases God. There have never been any great men or women of faith who did not tithe, going all the way back to Abraham himself. (See Genesis 14:20)

Chapter Six

The Roof of Fellowship

The roof of your house is fellowship with God. This is what it all comes down to, a personal relationship with the Creator. This is why we were created in the first place. To walk with Him, to talk with Him, to commune with Him. When you have an unbroken relationship with the Lord, no storms can hurt you. They will bounce off you and you will barely acknowledge them. Having fellowship with God is what it really means to be an overcomer.

Prayer, which is absolutely essential to our lives as Christians, becomes a two-way conversation instead of a ritualistic practice, a practice that feels like talking to a wall. The best illustration I can think of is when you call someone on the phone and get an answering machine. As you speak to it, it is very evident that you are not talking to a person. If the person you called picks up the phone in the middle of your call, the feeling is suddenly changed. You are now talking to a real person, not a machine. That is the difference in your prayer life when you are walking in fellowship with God.

The same can be said of reading His Word. It seems to become alive when you are in right standing with the Lord. It is the difference between reading the printed word, and reading the living Word.

You can read the same passage thirteen times, and come out with thirteen different nuggets of God's wisdom. When you read something that points out sin in your life, it is conviction, not condemnation. Condemnation was not God's plan.

"For God did not send His Son into the world to condemn the world, but to save the world through Him." (John 3:17 NIV)

Put up this roof, the Roof of Fellowship, keep it up, and maintain it. I found that these four walls,

Thanksgiving, Worship, Grace, and Tithe, were the areas I needed to work on personally to enable me to put up the Roof of Fellowship. If they are not up, the roof sort of collapses. I am not hearing His voice when I am acting in selfishness, envy, bitterness, murmuring, judgment of others, being offended, or not trusting in Him for my financial security. The evidence of the fruit of the Spirit starts to rot, so to speak. That evidence is your confident assurance that you are a child of the Living God. " … by this my Father is glorified, that you bear much fruit, and so prove to be my disciples." (John 15:8 ESV)

These four walls have helped me in so many other problem areas also. This is an on-going project, as I stated in the beginning. So much of the garbage of the world, the lies of the accuser, and the storms of life just fall away when these walls are built up and kept up.

Being found in fellowship with Him through all we face in this life will bring these seven words all born again believers should ache to hear: "Well done my good and faithful servant." (Matthew 25:23 KJV)

Summary

The Foundation

Do everything God's way. Seek first the Kingdom of God and His righteousness. Keep this as the absolute unchanging foundation to build up all aspects of your spiritual and natural walk, and you will not be tossed about by the storms of life. This approach will anchor you to the rock of His Word. If you truly learn how to do this in all things, victory over all darkness will be yours. It is the single most important attitude to have as a disciple of our Lord.

Wall One–Thanksgiving

Become a person of gratefulness to God in all things. He has made your path straight. He has redeemed you by His own blood. He walks with you throughout this life and faces all things with you. Do not give in to self-pity, envy, ungratefulness, and the misery that that the idolatry of self rewards you.

Thankfulness will produce the fruit of Joy; the Joy of the Lord.

Wall Two–Worship

Learn to worship the lord your God when you face your enemy, when you face your trial, and when you least feel like it. You will become an overcomer in all situations, and be a true worshipper in spirit.

Do not worship your situation, or give heed to the devil by murmuring and complaining. That will lead you to a depressed, overcome life, with no victory.

Worship will produce the fruit of Peace, the Peace of God that goes beyond our understanding. It will also produce patience and long suffering, and the ability to trust in God in all circumstances and situations. You will become a person of Faith; a person who pleases God.

Wall Three–Grace

Learn to forgive, as He has forgiven you. No matter what you see, no matter what anyone says or does to you, forgive them. Pay no heed to the accuser's voice. You will become a man or woman of great strength and endurance, one that the enemy cannot take out. No persecution or accusation will hold any weight against you. God will be able to trust you in ministry to others, and promote you in His Kingdom. Operating in grace and forgiveness will help you to keep your eyes on Jesus in a very unique way.

Grace will produce the fruit of Love; the Love of God for others, no matter how their 'humanity' treats you.

Wall Four–Tithe

Keep your finances in His hands. They are better hands than yours, no matter what you see in the natural. Trust in Him and keep His commandments. Don't worship the golden calf, as there is no security in it.

Tithing will start you on the road to a life of Faith; Faith that pleases God. Faith that says, "My life is yours Lord."

The Roof–Fellowship

This is our goal. This is His desire for you–a personal relationship with Him. With fellowship in place in your life, the Joy of the lord and the Peace that passes understanding, will reign. When fellowship with God is broken by us, everything just seems to start going wrong. Misery, worry, envy, loneliness, depression, and all other 'rewards' the great liar has in store for anyone listening and paying heed to what he says is the devil's reward. Satan is only interested in destroying you.

Fellowship with God will make praying a real conversation and communion time with Him, and reading the Word will be a delight, not a chore.

Guard your heart, and guard this fellowship dearly. Covet it above all else in life.

Authors Note

Some time ago I was listening to a sermon on sin. A sermon about how much God has forgiven us. How He has separated us as far from our sin as the east is from the west.

I immediately thought to myself, "Boy, there can't be a bigger distance than that!" The Lord spoke to me right then and explained to me that there is actually no distance at all between them. It was not a distance He told us about, but a direction. God, in His infinite wisdom, knows exactly how to word things.

Let us say that the west represents sin, and east represents righteousness. As you are traveling east, west is right behind you. You could travel east for 20 years or more, and all you have to do is stop, turn-around, and take a step. You are now going west once again. If there was distance between them, you could turn around and head west for some time, and would not be in sin because of the distance you had traveled. That is not how it works.

We need to head east, and keep heading east. There is absolute eternal security in heading east. Turn west, and no matter how much you have done, how much you have learned, how much you have experienced, or how well you have constructed your spiritual house, you are now headed west. You are now walking down off the rock and back to your old beach house.

Paul himself knew this, and wrote about it. He was concerned at the end that he would turn west, after leading so many to turn east.

> … I beat my body and make it my slave, so that after I have preached to others, I myself will not be disqualified for the prize.
>
> (I Corinthians 9:27 NIV)

of Christ; in order to be the light to the world, reflecting Jesus and not our own fallen sinful natures.

I found for me that no matter how hard I would try I could not foster the relationship with our Lord I needed in order to be the Christian I was meant to be. I could not maintain the level of fellowship preached about, no matter how hard I tried. As we bring up our children, we would like to teach them self-discipline, but we need to start off teaching them plain old discipline first. If we teach them how to behave, how to live, how to act, even though they do not understand why at that time, they will in time learn self-discipline. It will become such a part of them, that even if they depart from it, they will return to it, because they will know the truth. We can be the same way sometimes. Just as babes, we need to learn how to walk, how to talk, and how to act. Learn to put on the attitudes that Jesus had, so we can reflect Him to the world and live a victorious live here on earth. Lets not give authority to the enemy by paying heed to his lies, no matter how 'real' or 'true' they seem to our natural eyes. The enemy's lies will make you inconsistent, and keep you living in misery, depression, sickness, uncertainty, and defeat. Let's not let him win anymore! When we are walking, talking, thinking and acting God's way, the fellowship and growth we desire will not be such a big effort to try to maintain in our own strength, but will flow through us like a river of life.

May the Lord bless and keep you.

Sincerely,

Nathan

Biography

Nathan Lambshead was born in September of 1958, in Bangor, Maine, USA. His parents were called to the mission field in South Africa in 1964, where Nathan and his younger brother Peter were raised. Their mother, Marjory Ann, was murdered in 1987 during the unrest in South Africa. Their Father, Charles Frederick, stayed on as a missionary to the South African people for another 16 years. He died in 2003 in South Africa and went on to join his wife in glory.

Nathan settled in the United States in 1984. He lives in a rural town in southern New Hampshire with his wife Rebecca, and their son, Caleb.

He works at a commercial printer in New Hampshire, and runs a freelance graphic design company he started in 1997 called Goodnews Graphics. His brother Peter lives in South Africa with his wife Gail.

To contact the author: goodnews@ptcnh.net or info@goodnewsgraphics.biz

TATE PUBLISHING & *Enterprises*

Tate Publishing is commited to excellence in the publishing industry. Our staff of hightly trained professionals, including editors, graphic designers, and marketing personnel, work together to produce the very finest books available. The company reflects the philosophy established by the founders, based on Psalms 68:11,

"THE LORD GAVE THE WORD AND GREAT WAS THE COMPANY OF THOSE WHO PUBLISHED IT."

If you would like further information, please call
1.888.361.9473
or visit our website
www.tatepublishing.com

TATE PUBLISHING & *Enterprises*, LLC
127 E. Trade Center Terrace
Mustang, Oklahoma 73064 USA